Foundations of the Cross
and Other Bible Stories

Foundations of the Cross and Other Bible Stories

CYNTHIA ERLANDSON

RESOURCE *Publications* • Eugene, Oregon

FOUNDATIONS OF THE CROSS AND OTHER BIBLE STORIES

Copyright © 2024 Cynthia Erlandson. All rights reserved. Except for brief quotations in critical publications or reviews, no part of this book may be reproduced in any manner without prior written permission from the publisher. Write: Permissions, Wipf and Stock Publishers, 199 W. 8th Ave., Suite 3, Eugene, OR 97401.

Resource Publications
An Imprint of Wipf and Stock Publishers
199 W. 8th Ave., Suite 3
Eugene, OR 97401

www.wipfandstock.com

PAPERBACK ISBN: 979-8-3852-2516-3
HARDCOVER ISBN: 979-8-3852-2517-0
EBOOK ISBN: 979-8-3852-2518-7

VERSION NUMBER 07/02/24

Unless otherwise noted, Scripture quotations are taken from the New King James Version®. © Thomas Nelson

The first epigraph for "Passacaglia for Wind, Percussion, and Still Small Voice" is © The Teaching Company, 2006.

Cover art by Fr. Larry Lossing. ©The Parish Press, Inc. Used by permission.

"... having been built on the foundation of the apostles and prophets, Jesus Christ Himself being the chief cornerstone."
—Ephesians 2:20

CONTENTS

Preface | xi
Acknowledgments | xiii

FOUNDATIONS OF THE CROSS

I. The First Generation: Abraham Takes Up His Loss | 3
II. The Fear's Negation: Sarah Gives Birth to Isaac | 5
III. Faith's Confirmation: The Wood Is Laid Upon Isaac | 6
IV. The Birthright Usurpation: Jacob Supplants the First Time | 8
V. The Deceiver's Evacuation: Jacob Supplants the Second Time | 9
VI. The Transformation: Jacob Meets the Angels of Heaven | 11
VII. The Dream Sensation: Joseph Is Stripped of His Coat | 13
VIII. The Desolation: Jacob Is Shown Joseph's Coat | 16
IX. Predestination: Pharaoh's Kingdom Is Laid Upon Joseph | 18
X. The Condemnation: Joseph Is Stripped of his Royal Garments | 20
XI. Dream Interpretation: Joseph Rises a Second Time | 22
XII. The Revelation: Joseph Appears to His Brothers | 25
XIII. The Consolation: Jacob Is Reunited with Joseph | 28
XIV. Salvation: Christ Descends from Abraham | 30

OTHER BIBLE STORIES
I. Veiled: Figures of the True: Old Testament Stories

Earthbound Angels | 37
Noah's Prayer | 39
But Who Am I? | 42
Passacaglia for Wind, Percussion, and Still Small Voice | 44
Job's Request | 48
Dominus Regnavit | 50

All Flesh Is Grass | 51
David's Harp | 52
The Concert at the Fiery Furnace | 54
Babylon's Regret: A Survivor's Diary | 56

II. Revealed: The Things Concerning Himself: Old and New Testament Links

The Breath of Life: Dry Bones in Three Movements | 63
How Shall This Be? | 65
Nunc Dimittis | 67
If You Ask for Bread, Will He Give You a Stone? | 69
Two Variations on the Theme of Christ's Bride | 71
Four Variations on the Crown of Thorns | 73
The Lamb | 76
Are You the Coming One? | 77
Good Friday: "Let Me Die with the Philistines." | 80
Strange Blindness: A Play in Two Acts | 81
Morbid Joke | 84
The Donkey's Palm Sunday | 87
Easter Morning: Early Risers | 89
Partings | 91

III. Fulfilled: It Is Finished: New Testament Stories

Christmas with the Animals | 95
The Shepherds of the Night | 96
"And the Darkness Did Not Comprehend It." | 97
Sordid Signs | 98
Three Triptychs | 99
Three Days | 100
If You Are the Son of God | 102
Only One Wins the Prize | 104
The Man Born Blind | 106
A Psalm for Lazarus | 108
Judas' Kiss | 110
Thirty Pieces of Silver | 112
Twice and Thrice | 114

Triolet: Fear, Friends, Sheep | 115
Christ Before Pilate | 116
Pilate's Wife | 118
The Accusation | 119
Come Down | 121
Villanelle for Violins | 123
Easter, 2018: April Fool's Day | 125
Sepulchre | 126
Easter Matins: Meditations on Fabric, Flesh, and Stone | 128
Anticlimax | 132
Another Doubting Thomas | 133
Peter's Epiphany | 134
What Fire Is This? | 136

PREFACE

One of the things I'm most grateful for about my childhood is having grown up in a home and a church in which Bible reading was part of life. The first advantage this gave me was the obvious one of acquiring knowledge of the most profound and true story ever told. The second, though it came from the same source (the *King James Version*), didn't become obvious until much later. Yet all along, the beauty of its language had been working its way deeply into my mind, my soul, and even my body: a subconscious but strongly *felt* force of poetic rhythm akin to music. Long before I ever thought of writing poetry, this music of words was shaping the ways I thought and heard, and would eventually find expression in meter and rhyme. This influence was reinforced and intensified when I found my way into the Anglican Church by way of *The Book of Common Prayer*, from which, for over three decades, I've heard and felt the ringing of the same kind of exquisite verbal music. My life has been deepened greatly through this work of Christian literary art.

Foundations of the Cross and Other Bible Stories emerged as I began to hear the Testaments echoing each other, and to catch glimpses of "the mystery which has been hidden from ages and from generations, but now has been revealed to His saints." (Col 1: 26, NKJV) Living truths began to come to light: that "the household of God" has "been built on the foundation of the apostles and prophets, Jesus Christ Himself being the chief cornerstone..." (Eph 2: 19–20, NKJV)—and that the Law, the Prophets, and the Psalms all foretold Christ. (Luke 24: 44) In these poems, I have attempted to lead the reader, subtly, to hear these exciting echoes which reveal the Bible as one unified book.

The first part, *Foundations of the Cross*, presents fourteen short chapters that retell major events in salvation history, beginning with "The First Generation: Abraham Takes Up His Loss", and culminating with "Salvation: Christ Descends from Abraham". These chapters incorporate allusions meant to reveal times at which Old Testament persons and events foreshadow the life of Christ.

The second part, *Other Bible Stories*, is presented in three sections: *Veiled* narratives of the Old Testament (which "veil is taken away in Christ" [2 Cor 3: 13–14]) lead to *Revealed* reflections of "the things concerning Himself", linking the two Testaments (Luke 24: 27) and finally to the New Testament's proclamation of the *Fulfilled* prophecies of those who have "foretold these days." (Acts 3: 24)

ACKNOWLEDGMENTS

I am grateful to these publications for previously publishing the following poems:

First Things: All Flesh Is Grass

The Society of Classical Poets: Pilate's Wife; Sordid Signs (titled "The Eternal Design May Appear")

Forward in Christ magazine: Earthbound Angels; Dominus Regnavit; Another Doubting Thomas; Dust Before the Wind; Easter Morning: Early Risers

The North American Anglican: Two Variations on the Theme of Christ's Bride

The Catholic Poetry Room: Foundations of the Cross, Part I; The Lamb; A Psalm for Lazarus

I am deeply indebted to my husband Paul, who is an excellent poet, for his continuous constructive criticism of all of my poems, as well as his technical help preparing the manuscript. I am also grateful to biblical scholar Dan Lewis for reading, and making valuable suggestions for, the first ("Foundations of the Cross") section of this collection.

Foundations of the Cross

I. THE FIRST GENERATION: ABRAHAM TAKES UP HIS LOSS

> "And he went out, not knowing where he was going."
> —Heb 11:8

> "... but hope that is seen is not hope..."
> —Rom 8:24

It was not by human power that Sarah, bent
With barren decades, took the pilgrimage;
She only had her husband's cryptic word
That God had spoken, and that they were sent
(Her womb still void) to build a heritage
For non-existent heirs—how absurd
It sounded. Nor was it by sight he led
Her there; he'd been given no visible token
But the faraway stars. Not knowing where he went,
He slept below the light of those stars' unnumbered
Host, and dreamed about the singular nation
To which his wife would give birth one day. Encumbered
With faith—his heaviest load—in expectation
He gave a tithe, and was promised that his offspring
Would be slaves (a debatable blessing—
Dust of the earth, to be walked on,

Despised by Ishmael's pagan elder nation,
Until the covenanted generation
Which he would never see.)
                              His endurance test
Was Sarah's foreshadowing cross, and her bitter jest.
Having waited laughably long, still now unblessed
Among women, she swelled intensely with discontent
As the very air expanded expectantly:
Brisk breezes inflated the flocks of servants' tents;
They looked enlarged with laughter—seemed to mock
The woman's antique biologic clock.
Camels and cattle continually procreated;
A bountiful offering of fruit was generated
In fertile dirt, from which unseen offspring seemed
To cry out from the ground till her weary spirit screamed
From the deadly depths of envy's poison root
Ballooning below her skin as if it would burst.
By all appearances, she had been cursed.
While waiting for something unusual under the sun,
God's chosen patriarch who had no son
Disconcertedly blurted the overdue question
About the aging promise and its requisite relation
For which he had waited in seeming futility:
The wealth that his work, and the hope that his faith, had merited—
Friendship with God, and the land's fertility—
Still wearily waited to be inherited.

II. THE FEAR'S NEGATION: SARAH GIVES BIRTH TO ISAAC

> "... nor of the will of man, but of God."
>
> —JOHN 1:13

She was weaned off cynicism as she swelled
With the comic relief that arrived in the form of a child
Born to a father already a century old.
And despite the ninety years she'd had to see
How all man's labor leads to vanity,
Like mothers everywhere, she celebrated.
The sword that had always pierced her soul, she evaded,
Avoiding the vision of future slavery
To which her children's chosenness would doom them.
With deliberate irony, she named him Laughter,
Choosing for now to be blind to what was looming
For Abraham and Isaac not long after.

III. FAITH'S CONFIRMATION: THE WOOD IS LAID UPON ISAAC

> "... the one whom God blesses he curses in the same breath."
> —Soren Kierkegaard, *Fear and Trembling*

Believing, in spite of his torment, that Isaac would not
See corruption—he wouldn't return to Sarah bereft
Of their son—he buried his fear and trembling, and left
His wife behind, blind to the harrowing plan.
For a century he had believed without evidence, fought
With time, and against others' unbelief. Had it been vain?
And, what sort of horrendous reward, for all of his patience,
Was this waiting—once turned to laughter, but now to a knowing
Father's unbearable torture? What kept him going?
What, but the madness of hope, when his life seemed cursed?

Now the promised son, Isaac, upon whose prolonged life
Depended his father's appointment as Father of Nations,
Suddenly sees the silver slaughtering knife.
Who sinned—this young boy, or his parents—that he was ordained
To play such a horrible part in a drama designed
To confirm agony as God's way? One would rather be blind
Than to see the unbearable end of their destination.
After this, could the substitute ram calm their great consternation?

Or, was this spiritual wound irreparable, leaving
A terminal limp to a father continually grieving?
Did the son, who saw the sharp edge of God's revelation,
Accept his role in the plan, although uncertain
Whether he could endure its intolerable burden?

IV. THE BIRTHRIGHT USURPATION: JACOB SUPPLANTS THE FIRST TIME

> "Do not labor for the food which perishes..."
> —JOHN 6:27

Esau, the short-sighted twin, only thinks about now.
Having worked through the heat of the day with his arrow and bow,
His hunger demanding immediate gratification
(Blinding him to the present transparent temptation),
He follows forceful olfactory sensations.
"What profit has a man for all his labor,
If not for food to fill his empty belly?
A dead man won't inherit one thing, will he?
Here—see what good the Birthright does you, Grabber."
His endowment as firstborn shall surely die; thus he
Betrays all generations of his family
By refusing to ponder beyond the immediate meal.
He smells the red stew that is good for food, and he eats.
But his eyes are not opened; he already knows good and evil,
And chooses the latter; his surly mood defeats
Him. He takes the forbidden food, selling his soul,
And Jacob, again, has grasped his brother's heel.

V. THE DECEIVER'S EVACUATION: JACOB SUPPLANTS THE SECOND TIME

> "... there are wicked men to whom it happens according to the work of the righteous."
> —Eccl 8:14

> "... not of works, but of him who calls..."
> —Rom 9:11

God having negated the Birthright (as he will despise
The shedding of sheep's and goats' blood in sacrifice),
Jacob counts the blessing as his to steal.
Rebekah, knowing her plot needs a veil, supplies
Her son with goats' clothing, while cooking a sacred meal.
Jacob—presuming on God to hide his eyes
While he dishonors his father, in hairy disguise—
Gives God the credit for the savory platter of lies
By which he advances his plan. Rebekah's scheme,
And his plots, are woven on a serpentine
Warp of deception, a colorful garment passed on
As a legacy to each sinner under the sun.
Isaac, with overcast eyes and a father's pained heart
Eclipsed with sad decades of watching his warring sons,
Acts—as a priest—by faith and not by sight,

Trusting the feast served by this false acolyte,
Accepting this sheep in goats' clothes God has placed on the right.

VI. THE TRANSFORMATION: JACOB MEETS THE ANGELS OF HEAVEN

"... you have struggled with God and with men, and have prevailed."
—GEN 32:28

"... My strength is made perfect in weakness."
—2 COR 12:9

With Esau seeing red from the blessing he'd lost,
Jacob knows that, by taking the firstborn's place, he has crossed
The line. While his brother is raising cain, full-fed,
He wastes no time dodging Abel's fate, and has fled.
Having wrestled the blessing and birthright away from his brother,
Now exhausted, the thief and deceiver attempts to find rest
On a stone which, unknown to him, is the gate of heaven.
Far from rebuking him for his false witness, God rather
Shows him a vision, and tells him what he will be given.
His baffling reward (perhaps also his retribution)
Is to be divinely appointed unfortunate father
Of numberless sinner-descendants multiplying
And (just like their father) thieving, betraying, lying,
Envying, fighting, given to fornication,
Blaspheming, glutting, bent on intoxication,
Begetting sons of depravity's sorrows who,

Enslaved by pagan nations, must struggle and writhe
Toward an unseen time when some purpose for their pain
And their inbred crookedness might be made plain.
Unaccountably grateful, he promises God a tithe.

Years later this ancient-day prodigal son, now rich,
This time escaping from Laban, wrestles again,
And again receives a blessing—but now from a Man
Who can't pin him down, but finally has to wrench
His hip out of joint. This permanent dislocation,
Though not a propitious sign for the start of a nation,
Accompanies the twisting of Jacob's name
In its socket, as well: the momentous new designation
Of Israel is given to him. He is one and the same
With the chosen tribes of the God who seems always inclined,
Absurdly, to seek and to save the lame and the blind.

VII. THE DREAM SENSATION: JOSEPH IS STRIPPED OF HIS COAT

"Then last of all he sent his son to them, saying, 'They will respect my son.'"
—MATT 21:37

"Yes, his soul draws near the Pit, and his life to the executioners."
—JOB 33:22

Among the twelve brothers, the question of who will be greatest
Is answered, without being asked. Jacob's son of old age
Swells with dreams of many colors he tells to his outraged
Rivals, though knowing already how strong their hate is.
If the dreams had showed him more, he could have alerted
His father: "A little while and you shall not see me—
But a little while again, and you shall see me."
Or, if he had known what pain his boldly-asserted
Supremacy would cause him, he might have forbidden
Himself to cast his pearls before the dozen,
Keeping God's secret announcement to him hidden
To ponder in his heart. Yet, if he had chosen
To go back, by a dream, a different way—
Instead of brazen-facedly explaining
How every star would bow to him some day—

It might have seemed that he would have been gaining
His life, but losing the world he was meant to be saving.

Now Jacob, assuming that they will respect his son,
Sends Joseph to the workers, wearing the sign
Of his status. But rather than casting lots for it,
They mar the robe's beauty with goats' blood, and find a pit
In which to imprison this heir of outrageous dreams,
So that the inheritance will be theirs. "Hail, king
Of the sheaves and the heavenly bodies! See how your schemes
Come to nothing! Ha—now let's hear you prophesy!
We have dreamed that it is expedient you should die
For the peace of the family. All we must do is bring
This bloody coat home, to clear ourselves. One lie
Will remove the thorn from our flesh. We're just getting even.
After all, what's one son to our father? He still has eleven.

So Joseph, both scapegoat and sheep, descends to the pit
With his lifetime of self-congratulations, his wit
(Which he had supposed a delightful oblation to God),
And his ego descending with him into the mud,
While his murderous older brothers are marked for protection,
Even as the coat cries out with the blameless goat's blood
(With which Jacob will be repaid for all his deceptions.)
Although blind in the pit, Joseph will not (for now) see corruption,
Because into Egypt God has called this son.

When the twelfth is gone, the eleven betrayers take bread
And eat, making plans for the kill. But God holds back their hands,
And lets this cup pass from Joseph—his life is saved.
In this strange plot twist, he will instead be enslaved.

Twenty pieces of silver: the prophecy's unhappy trap
Starts a four-hundred years' episode in a foreign land
For the patriarchs' future descendants. Not one understands
The significance of these perplexing, momentous events:
How their lacerated relations are being engraved
On the fate of their nation. The brother whose arrogant taunts
Had filled them with fury, was crucial for them to be saved:
Their family, from impending Egyptian dearth;
And ultimately, from sin, the whole earth.

VIII. THE DESOLATION: JACOB IS SHOWN JOSEPH'S COAT

> "... the Almighty has dealt very bitterly with me."
> —Ruth 1:20

> "... man, though in honor, does not remain; he is like the beasts that perish."
> —Ps 49:12

"Behold and see if there be any likely resemblance
Of this garment to Joseph's. Have you a clear remembrance?
It would probably be impossible, with these stains,
To recognize it, in any case . . ."
                                        Dreadful pains
Seized the father, who tore his clothes at the sight of the coat
(Not seeing that some of his sons appeared to gloat).
Then Jacob was heard loudly weeping for his child,
Refusing all comfort, living only to mourn.
Not one of the brothers admitted that they had beguiled
Their father, who thought that his favorite had been torn
By what man has no advantage over: the wild
Beasts; men perish, as brutes do, in vanity.
Yet man is more cursed, with the lasting infirmity
Of the battle of hatred and love, from which beasts are free.

It is this that makes man desire to return his dust
To the earth as it was, and his spirit to God who gave it.
Jacob has seen great affliction; yet he must
Continue allowing his soul to be harrowed to save it,
With sorrow that razes his heart as if to engrave it
With grief, from which nothing but death can give relief.

IX. PREDESTINATION: PHARAOH'S KINGDOM IS LAID UPON JOSEPH

> "He sent a man before them—Joseph—who was sold as a slave . . . He made him lord of his house, and ruler of all his possessions."
> —Ps 105:17, 21

> ". . . whoever desires to become great among you, let him be your servant."
> —Matt 20:26

> "Joseph is a fruitful bough . . ."
> —Gen 49:22

Having kept all his dreams
And pondered them in his heart,
Perhaps puzzled about his part
In God's mysterious schemes,
Joseph accepts his burden
Which had started in the pit.
He had lost his life to find it,
Had given up being certain
Of what God's unwieldy will meant,
Or how the dreams' fulfillment

Would come about, since his family
Could hardly find him now.

How peculiar of Pharaoh's officer to choose
Precisely the man whom God had already predestined,
And not to harden his heart, or to abuse
The one that God was secretly starting to use
(As future Pharaohs would hurt his descendants, oppressing
Them four-hundred years—until Moses—and then refusing
To free them.) Without the stellar audience now
Which Joseph had been promised in his visions,
He still begins to be the fruitful bough
Of the family tree that his father will one day envision.

X. THE CONDEMNATION: JOSEPH IS STRIPPED OF HIS ROYAL GARMENTS

> "... He was numbered with the transgressors ..."
> —Isa 53:12

> "There is a vanity which occurs on earth, that there are just men to whom it happens according to the work of the wicked; again, there are wicked men to whom it happens according to the work of the righteous..."
> —Eccl 8:14

"Behold and see the garment of this Hebrew!
He left it with me. Don't you recognize it?"
Thus, as the adulterous woman would devise it,
It happens that she, the wicked, is accorded
The wage of the righteous, while Joseph is rewarded
With the fruit of evil which to the wicked is due,
As if he had picked it, forbidden, from a bough
Of a sacred tree. Absurdly, staying pure
Brings the master's wrath. Now Joseph must endure
The vanity of trying to follow God's scheme
When it seems to mock one's supposedly God-given dream—
When it seems in vain to keep God's commands, since his plan
Does not appear to favor the righteous man.

He probably wonders if there is a logical reason
Why he had nearly died in a pit, and then risen,
If only to fall a second time, buried in prison.
Or maybe he speculates whether this all comes from casting
His lot with these pagans—though he had not cast his pearls
Before Potiphar's wife, or broken any rules.
Unjustly bound, he refuses to see this as wasting
His talent. He simply serves other men who are here
Instead of fretting about what seems unfair.
Thus, Joseph goes not up to joy without first feeling pain;
And walking, once again, in the way of his loss,
He enters not into glory before life's dross
Has tempted him to feel it is all in vain.
For man will be tempted to languish, whatever he's done,
And will not be spared much anguish under the sun.

XI. DREAM INTERPRETATION: JOSEPH RISES A SECOND TIME

> "... Oh Lord, I pray, send now prosperity."
> —Ps 118:25

> "And whoever desires to be first among you, let him be your slave..."
> —Matt 20:27

> "Bring my soul out of prison, that I may praise Your name..."
> —Ps 142:7

> "... Your young men shall see visions, Your old men shall dream dreams."
> —Acts 2:17

Tenaciously as autumn's last brown leaf
Clings to its branch through wind and heavy rain,
Joseph holds fast to his dream about his sheaf,
Believing that, at the right time, he will regain
What he's lost, and other sheaves will bow to his—
Not for his honor, but for God's purposes.
In the meantime, he serves his companions. Even here
He gains people's trust, and rises to overseer.

One morning he reads in two prisoners' faces a fear
Too profound to pass over. These men have also had dreams,
Full of bread-baskets, birds, Pharaoh's cup, and some grapes and vines.
An experienced dreamer, he knows these visions for signs
Which reveal tiny fragments of God's enigmatic designs.
But unlike Joseph's, these dreams would come true in three days.
Prophetically, he reveals both the good and the bad:
The cup of prison would pass from the butler; the bread
Was the flesh of the baker—in three days, he would be dead.
"Put in a good word for me to the king when
You're serving in the palace once again.
I am not guilty; it is for nothing I've done
That I am here. I am of the Hebrew nation,
And was stolen long ago from my native land,
And now I am under the same condemnation
As if I were the thief. But I've done nothing wrong
That I should have been imprisoned for so long."
Soon it happens as Joseph has said, and as God had planned:
The baker is hanged, and God will let
The butler return to his post and forget
About Joseph. Somehow, it is not yet
His time to rise from prison; so still he stays,
Pondering God's inscrutable delays.

Two years later, the butler abruptly remembers him when
His king has a double dream: first cows, and then corn
That devour their fellows. The skeletal and forlorn
Ones consume (but to no effect) the strong specimens.
Pharaoh, tormented by these ominous scenes,
Troubles his magi to tell him what it all means.

Because of their ultimate failure to be true seers,
They take Joseph out of prison, and let him go
To the palace of Pharaoh. Perhaps he could calm the king's fears.
After all his years of longsuffering captivity,
He's prepared to begin his public ministry
At thirty years old—his second triumphal entry.
But, "Weep for yourselves and for your posterity,
For Egypt shall lack for food," is his prophecy.
"The nation shall surely die, unless Pharaoh elects
A man to take charge of the grain. He will have to collect
And store it, to turn back this dreadful destiny."
So Joseph creates his own job description, and finds
His life, after having seemed for so long to have lost it.
He is clothed in a royal robe, which likely reminds
Him of one from his past, and of how much that one had cost:
It had goaded his pride, and incited his brothers' resentment,
Without which he wouldn't be here. Though he hadn't yet guessed,
Their immanent flight into Egypt will prevent
His family's extinction. Yet a little while
And they shall see him here, where he'd been sent.

XII. THE REVELATION: JOSEPH APPEARS TO HIS BROTHERS

> "But we were hoping that it was He who was going to redeem Israel."
> —LUKE 24:21

Having come home from Egypt with coins that appeared
As if by malignant magic in their sacks,
They assume they are thought of as thieves, and therefore fear
To return. Ironically, they are also held back
By their youngest brother—or rather their father, who grieves
Endlessly for Rachel's other child—
His favorite—whom he probably believes
Had come to harm by these brothers, his story untold.
But blessed are those who hunger; for hunger demands
To be accommodated. And so, the command
From the ruler of Egypt, who told them to bring their brother,
Had to be followed so that, in God's ultimate plan—
Even while blind to it—they could seek the dead
Among the living.   Now, away from their father—
From whom they'd had to hide, for so long, their sin
Against Joseph—they walk along the road with dread,
Reasoning and brooding together under the sun
Of things they now regretted that they had done:

How they had, in fact, been guilty of thievery
When, for his vanity, they had delivered
Their brother to a life of slavery,
Not caring for the grief of their gray-haired father
Over the loss of the son he had highly favored.
They speak what they are all thinking, what Ruben had said
In Egypt: that their betrayal was known by God,
And that he now required their brother's blood
Of them—and, indeed, justly. They wonder whether
God is, or the stars are, requiting them—little knowing
That they are Joseph's stars, and will soon be bowing
To him once again. Their old sibling rivalry
Will be irrelevant when they know it is he
Who will establish the hope of their family.
But they've had no vision of angels to tell them the news
That he is alive.
      Penitent, they are determined
To return the silver coins, even if accused,
Hoping that such a cup of suffering
Will be taken from them.

      When Joseph sees Benjamin,
His heart starts burning intensely within him.
Vanishing from their sight, Joseph weeps,
His whole family history coming up from the deeps
Of his heart. But their eyes are restrained; they do not know him.
Even in the service at the table,
When he orders them by ages, they are unable
To recognize the one that they'd betrayed,
Until he himself at last stands in their midst
And says, "Peace be to you. Be not afraid.

See me; touch me; know I am your brother.
Tell me now, I pray you, of our father."
Although his words at this strange moment seem
Like idle tales, their hearts beat as though they'd seen
A ghost. Catching their breath, they remember his dreams,
And their eyes are opened; their hearts beat more quickly, more loudly;
Fear of vengeance overcomes the eleven.
But he tells them not to blame themselves. "What seems
Unjust, is made good by God. I acted proudly;
Yet he chose me to save this land, and prepare a haven
For us. Therefore, ought I not to have suffered these things?
I have not come to destroy you, but to fulfill
These events that have happened according to God's own will,
And have now ascended to this very place
To save many alive; else surely you would have died.
You are forgiven; you knew not what you did.
As for me, I now understand the things
That separated us. You must retrace
Your steps, and tell our father I'm alive,
And bring him back with you. Here we will live,
We and our children. This was God's design,
Which far exceeded any plots of mine.

XIII. THE CONSOLATION: JACOB IS REUNITED WITH JOSEPH

> "Almighty God, whose most dear Son went not up to joy but first he suffered pain, and entered not into glory before he was crucified; Mercifully grant that we, walking in the way of the cross, may find it none other than the way of life and peace; through the same thy Son Jesus Christ our Lord. Amen."
> —The Book of Common Prayer, Collect for the Monday before Easter

> "... And Jacob's heart fainted, for he believed them not."
> —Gen 45:26 (KJV)

The eleven return, and tell all these things to Jacob,
But their words seem to him like impossible, idle tales.
By this time his son, and his hope, have been dead for two decades;
To roll the stone from his heart now, might cause it to fail.
He knows not what his heart does—shocked with such a delayed
Resurrection—so long has he walked in the grueling way
Of the loss, with a sword still piercing his spirit and soul.
As far as his home in the east is from Egypt's west,
So far-fetched is this scheme from any he could have guessed,
This bewildering news that he trembles too much to believe.
Still unable to see straight, he finds himself packing to leave,

Feeling younger already. His life perhaps hasn't been wasted.
His mind's eye imagines it, from the dreadful day
When the brothers brought back Joseph's coat with mock dismay.
That day had darkened his vision, had all but exhausted
His wrestling spirit and body. His outlook is altered
While his mind adapts its perspective. Through God's surprise,
Because of a tragedy, all of them now would be sheltered
From famine. He sees how all people are paralyzed
With desire to get first to joy without suffering pain.
He had to lose Joseph's life, and his own, to find
Their purpose—to which he had been, until now, blind;
His past loss is his family's present and future gain.

Unlike Abraham, they would know exactly where
They were going. Saved by a happy dislocation
From the famine, so that they would not surely die,
They would carry on God's appointed generations.
So Jacob awakes from his nightmare; his spirit revives,
And he knows that from this time on, he will never grieve
Again, knowing that Joseph is still alive.
Yet a little while, he'll see his son's face;
Another while, he will have run his race.

XIV. SALVATION: CHRIST DESCENDS FROM ABRAHAM

> "And if you are Christ's, then you are Abraham's seed, and heirs according to the promise."
>
> —GAL 3:29

> "So all the generations from Abraham to David are fourteen generations, from David until the captivity in Babylon are fourteen generations, and from the captivity in Babylon until the Christ are fourteen generations."
>
> —MATT 1:17

Generations later, another Joseph
Had followed in the footsteps of Abraham, Isaac,
Jacob, and Joseph on their Egyptian route
Along the foundation that finally had enough
Ancestral history: forty-two layers thick.
This unexpected trip had come about
Because his promised bride had answered "yes"
To a challenge that counted him in. So now, without
Any way to know they were walking the way of the cross—
Or to comprehend why God would raise up Herod
To place this Son of his age in mortal danger—
This Joseph also left his home. He hurried

To Egypt with his family. This was stranger
Than all he'd known—except God's startling voice
That had told him his virgin wife would be a mother.

She may have thought about Sarah's inconceivable
Conception, while Joseph remembered the sacrifice
That God had required of Isaac's elderly father.
Looking up, perhaps they remembered the unbelievable
Promise of Abraham fathering many nations—
People as numerous as the uncountable stars—
Or pondered Joseph's dream: the constellation
Of family bowing to him.
                        Soon, Herod's fears
Were enflamed with rage; his sage astronomers
Had sought God's wisdom through complex calculations,
Then followed this single star to His singular Son
Without coming back with the requisite information
Herod needed for a planned assassination.

Joseph and Mary, unable to dream of the scope
Of the part that they played in God's bewildering scheme,
Returned by another dream, nursing fear and hope,
Unaware, as they went, of the future crucifixion
That would draw their son's blood and lay the final foundation
Upon which is built his people's eternal salvation.

Other Bible Stories

I

Veiled
Figures of the True: Old Testament Stories

> "... unlike Moses, who put a veil over his face so that the children of Israel could not look steadily at the end of what was passing away ... For until this day the same veil remains unlifted in the reading of the Old Testament, because the veil is taken away in Christ."
>
> —2 COR 3:13–14

EARTHBOUND ANGELS

> "So He drove out the man; and He placed cherubim at the east of the garden of Eden, and a flaming sword which turned every way, to guard the way to the tree of life."
>
> —GEN 3:24

We are the guards of Eden's garden gate—
Earthbound, brought down from our exalted state,
Commissioned to prevent man's further quest
For paradise on earth, which the distressed
Eve and Adam left as spoiled terrain.
The fallen ones had seen their fault too late,
Belittled God's great gift, lost their estate,
In vain had rued their effort to equate
Themselves with him—which utmost sin created
This present madness: every human pain,
And our position here, where we must wait,
Ensuring that this garden's barricaded.
We're not the fallen ones from Satan's train;
Yet we're pedestrians on terrestrial ground.
Our wings are motionless in earth's time, bound
Behind us, as this garden gate's bound fast.
Our swords flash north to south and east to west,
Blazing with our vehement desire

To be set free from gravity, to fly
From sky to earth once more, from earth to sky
From day to night till he—exalted higher
Than men and angels—turns all wrong to right.
For that great day, both men and angels wait;
Till then, we stand on guard at Eden's gate.

NOAH'S PRAYER

> "And the Lord was sorry that He had made man on the earth, and He was grieved in His heart."
>
> —Gen 6:6

> "For the earth will be filled with the knowledge of the glory of the Lord, as the waters cover the sea."
>
> —Hab 2:14

Dear God, these people think that I'm a madman.
I sympathize—not just since they'll be dead men
Before too long—but since they are amused
That I am building something that will float,
While everything around us is so dry.
It seems their point of view could be excused;
I'm quite perplexed myself (though I don't doubt
The flood is coming). But I wonder why
It once was worth it to you to invent
Such disappointing images of you,
When all along you knew we'd be this way.
It's understandable you would repent
Of having made us—but then, why do you
Want to start again with just a few?
Because of Eve and Adam's fruitless try

To gain omniscience for humanity,
Which doomed us all to such insanity,
Wouldn't future people just continue
To be defiant, arrogant, unruly?

I'm pounding nails, but can't strike out this thought:
Just as the waters which will clothe the sea
That you have prophesied so long to me,
So evil always clothes humanity.
And so, I can't help wondering: just what
Will life on earth be like after this water
Comes down? Will coming generations then be better,
Less rebellious, more inclined to good?
Or will the tale repeat—will mankind rot
As we, till now, have done? I pray this cloud-
Burst of falling water you call rain
Absolves us from the Fall, makes people clean.
But I confess, I think that it will not;
I fear that we will struggle on in vain,
Continually tossed and wrecked upon
The stormy waves of vice for which we thirst,
And in its raging deluge be immersed.

Forgive me and my grumbling family,
Who lack the virtue of humility,
For questioning your wisdom while we wait
With thirsty hearts for you to re-create
The world.
      And then, at its baptismal rite,
Give us the faith that, someday, you'll erase
Our exile from the garden, and the damage

Humanity has wreaked upon your image.
Saturate the whole world with the knowledge
Of you, as waters cover every trace
Of sea. Help us to trust your flood of grace
To make us into a more godly race.

BUT WHO AM I?

> "But Moses said to God, 'Who am I that I should go to Pharaoh, and that I should bring the children of Israel out of Egypt?'"
> —Exod 3:11

God, did I hear you right? Did you tell me
(But who am I?) to lead these people out
Of Egypt? I'm not one to disagree;
In fact, I'm very slow of tongue—but
I know myself quite well; I'm not the sort
Of person for this job. Humans are not
My forte. All my life's experience
Is with these sheep. With men, I don't know what
To say. I'm sure I never could convince
This mob to go. I lack the eloquence.
I am an introvert. Nobody listens
To my ideas. I don't want to be
A head-of-state who gives commands. I am
Not one who understands psychology.
If I tried this, they'd all be asking me
How ever did I come up with this scam,
And anyway, who do I think I am?
And I am very certain they will sense
My fear, and laugh at me. They will not mince

Their insults when I tell that that I AM
Has sent me. They'll hear blasphemy, and either
They'll kill me, or at best they'll say they'd rather
Not go. I'm not your man. Please send another.

PASSACAGLIA FOR WIND, PERCUSSION, AND STILL SMALL VOICE

> "In a passacaglia, the theme is a structural rather than a surface element, a metaphor for the invisible hand of God controlling the rich chaos of the everyday."
>
> —Robert Greenberg, *How to Listen to and Understand Great Music* (The Great Courses, © The Teaching Company 2006)

> "... And behold, the Lord passed by, and a great and strong wind tore into the mountains and broke the rocks in pieces the before the Lord, but the Lord was not in the wind; and after the wind an earthquake, but the Lord was not in the earthquake; and after the earthquake a fire, but the Lord was not in the fire; and after the fire a still small voice."
>
> —I Kgs 19:11–12

Tremble O savage ravaging wind tremble O wind at the presence of God.
Blast boldly like trumpets, unmuted, in gusts;
Break eardrums with brassy fortissimo whispers;
Lash reeds; crack wood; break rocks; drive dust
From the face of the prophet. Blow soil from the eyes
That are blinded by clouds of fear. Revise
His blurry vision; dislodge the flurry

Of turmoil between his tone-deaf ears,
And silence his speech stirred by stormy years
Of valid vexation and turbulent toil.

Elijah, what are you doing here, your thoughts in a whirlwind of futile fury,
Your words (although thwarted, blown back down your throat) like hysterical hurricanes
                blocking your ears,
Your anger vibrating with vehement vengeance, confusing my plans with your frustrated hurry?
Yes, you have been zealous as blustering wind to speak my truth—yet you can't hear
Me through the crescendo of your rage. Take the mutes from your ears. Spit out the gravel
Without any words. Shake off the storm's stubble. Prepare yourself for a noiseless revival.
Attune your mind to a quieter sound
And listen intensely until you can hear
(I am not in the wind)
Until you can hear
        until you can hear
               until you can hear only me.

Shudder O shivering quavering earth shudder O earth at the presence of God.
Convulse, dense terra firma—shake
And gasp; speed your pulse. Stout
Dry land, crack into sand. Quake,
Strong mountains; rupture ego. Break,
Unbending rocks: ransack and rout
Decrepit virtues petrified;

Uproot the ancient wood; wrack
And ravage settled bedrock pride.

Elijah, what are you doing here, sleeping under the juniper tree,
Your nightmares throbbing (though rattled by fear) with your vigilant plans to overthrow
The pagan foe who overthrow my altars? Wake up, Elijah. I see
That you are very jealous for me, and quake with outrage for my sake.
But your dreams are too loud and too full of vibration. Still your mind; cease to stake
The earth on your efforts. I, only, make the earth to shake, the wind to blow.
Not tempests nor tyrants can break my control. My altars cannot be altered by men.
I make men quake. I wreck their plans. I am not in this noise, though I make the earth roll.
I am here. Can you hear? Take your ear from the ground
And listen for a different sound
Until you can hear
        until you can hear
                until you can hear only me.
Crackle O blazing razing fire crackle O fire at the presence of God.
Quiver with furious fervor. Incite
To percussive applause dry, frenzied leaves.
Lacerate the wind. Ignite
This one who wakes incensed—who grieves,
Indignant and fully infuriated
That judgment's infernos are greatly belated.
Incinerate his cynical prayer.
Enlighten his dimsighted view. Excite
Miraculous imaginings

Of the final triumph forbearance brings.

Elijah, what are you doing here, vibrating like leaves in this kindling wind—
Like soil on a fault-line—your countenance burning like igneous rock shaped by molten mourning?
Do you think vice is something new under the sun? A volcanic eruption of wrath will not bend
Evil men to your wishes. Their arrogant speeches
Won't stop me from healing earth's fire-filled breaches.
I hold all its corners, the strength of its hills.
Entwined winds and flames shape themselves to my will.
I countenance earth-shaking tyrants until
That day when I choose to breathe furious coals
—Beside which earth's blazing injustices pale—
And weigh in my heaven-sized, earth-shrinking scale
—In which all of your rages, though well-founded, fail—
The winds of the earth and the fire of men's souls.

JOB'S REQUEST

> "Oh, that You would hide me in the grave, that You would conceal me until Your wrath is past..."
>
> —JOB 14:13

A wiser man than I once said the day
Of death is better than the day of birth.
And furthermore, he said, the one who never
Saw the sun is luckiest of all.

Behold and see if there is any way
My suffering has ever on the earth
Been equaled. While I scratch my boils and shiver,
God, you seem indifferent to my soul.

The house of mourning's better than the feasts
And revelries of rich men. I would trade
All that I ever had for just a stable
In which to hide till this infirmity

Has passed. I'm lower than the lowest beasts.
I'm mocked by so-called friends, who have betrayed
Me. Why am I forsaken? I'm unable
To last much longer in this misery.

I used to think that what I sowed, I'd reap.
Now all I have to sow is my own corpse.
To live in holiness is vanity,
It seems; there's no reward in being just.

This life's intolerable. Out of the deep
I call to you; your lack of answer warps
Whatever I have left of sanity.
I'd rather that my flesh return to dust.

Nowhere is there help for me. Your arrows
Stick in my rotted flesh. Can this compare
Favorably with non-existence? More
Than this I cannot take. I need some rest.

I'm innocent, yet languish here, where sorrows
Will never cease—where I can only roar
In agony. I've nothing left to live for.
Please end my grief, and grant my last request:

Release me from this wretched life you gave.
I ask no more. Just let me breathe my last.
Oh, that you would hide me in the grave,
And would conceal me till your wrath is past.
Now in your mercy, grant me this, I pray,
Almighty One, who gives and takes away.

DOMINUS REGNAVIT

> "The Lord is King, be the people never so impatient;
> he sitteth between the Cherubim, be the earth never so unquiet."
>
> —Ps 99:1 (Coverdale)

High over all the mad, complaining people
Impatient with his much-too-patient waiting,
Between the cherubim, the King is sitting.
He's watched them try to steal his throne, parading
Themselves as gods, since Adam stole the apple.
He's heard them all continuously grapple
Against each other, each the other hating.
Though all earth's chaos is of their creating,
They rage at their Creator-King, equating
What he should do with what they want. They riot
In vain while still he sits, and does his bidding,
Be all the people never so unquiet.

ALL FLESH IS GRASS

> "When the ungodly are green as the grass, and when all the workers of wickedness do flourish, then shall they be destroyed forever; but thou, Lord, art the Most Highest forevermore."
>
> —Ps 92:7 (Coverdale)

> "In the morning it is green, and groweth up; but in the evening it is cut down, dried up, and withered."
>
> —Ps 90:6 (Coverdale)

When haughty lawless scoundrels with their boorish
Intrigues appear, like morning's grass, to neither
Be sickly nor in scarcity, but flourish
In brightest greens, while humble people wither
Like faded blades cut down and left to feed
Rogues' evil schemes—compost upon their vice—
One thinks perhaps to trade the Christian creed
For, "Some by virtue fall, and others rise
By sin." Malignant overgrowth of weeds
Appears to suffocate, with strong-willed roots,
The fairest fields and flowers, and all seeds
Except seeds of frustration, fear and doubt—
Until the evening mowers intervene,
Cut down the proud, and leave God's people green.

DAVID'S HARP

> "And it came to pass, when the evil spirit from God was upon Saul, that David took an harp, and played with his hand: so Saul was refreshed, and was well, and the evil spirit departed from him."
> —I Sam 16:23 (KJV)

> "I will incline mine ear to the parable, and show my dark speech upon the harp."
> —Ps 49:4 (Coverdale)

Provide me with a talented musician—
A harpist of extraordinary skill.
Perhaps the music's lyric language will
Relieve me of this evil apparition
That haunts me with a dissonant distress.
There is no sorcery or medicine
To remedy the pain my head is in,
Or soothe my soul, like harp-strings that express
An eloquent and calming composition.

True harpists' hands are moved by angels' hands.
Although a mortal only understands
In part the instrument's sublime expressions,
Its sounds speak to my spirit's intuitions.

This otherworldly cure for my condition
Uncannily suppresses all demonic
Dominion with its elegant harmonic
Healing of the heart and soul—a sonic
Cure from heaven's choir—the perfect tonic.

THE CONCERT AT THE FIERY FURNACE

> "O sages standing in God's holy fire
> As in the gold mosaic of a wall,
> Come from the holy fire, perne in a gyre,
> And be the singing-masters of my soul."
>
> —William Butler Yeats, *Sailing to Byzantium*

> "I see four men loose, walking in the midst of the fire; and they are not hurt, and the form of the fourth is like the Son of God."
>
> —Dan 3:25

The king—determined that all hell will freeze
Before he lets one person get away
With failing to fall down on face and knees
To him, as if he is a deity—
Heats up his private hell without delay.
Music of many kinds accompanies
This entertainment: Three wise men are bound
And tossed into the tyrant's furnace. They
Move gracefully, unharmed. The splendid sound
Of cornetts, flutes, harps, psaltery, and lyre—
The royal orchestra—is all but drowned
In loud percussive crackles of the fire.

The sages hear its furious sizzling music,
To which, in mystic calm, they slowly dance.
Spectators are surprised by a mosaic
Of moving parts: three men spin in a gyre—
Then suddenly, a Fourth one walks among
Them, whose unearthly golden countenance
Outshines the fire; while all the fire's tongues,
In godlike language, sing angelic songs.
The King (whose tongue has never stopped) springs from
His throne; at last he knows he's not as strong
As God. His conscience beaten like a drum,
As if he's seen the true Byzantium,
He shouts, "There's one more! And his golden form
Is like the Son of God! To him belongs
All power and an everlasting kingdom!
His glory and his might are truly fearsome!
To every generation his great wisdom
Is manifest. You men, whose first desire
Is serving your true God whatever dire
Things happen to you—Come from that frail fire
That cannot carry out my royal ire.
No other god is able to deliver
Like this. All men should worship him forever."

BABYLON'S REGRET: A SURVIVOR'S DIARY

> "And we might have a little heed
> Of what Belshazzar couldn't read."
>
> —Edwin Arlington Robinson, *The Voice of Age*

> "... the fingers of a man's hand appeared and wrote opposite the lampstand on the plaster of the wall of the king's palace ... Now all the king's wise men came, but they could not read the writing ..."
>
> —Dan 5:5, 8

Prologue

In hindsight, those prophetic floating fingers—
Apparently detached from some god's hand—
Were fitting for our plastered state; the figures
They wrote, a sign of our disfigured land.

Oblivious to the vast extent of decay
We'd brought our culture to—and dissipated
Beyond our eyes' ability to read
(We hadn't read much lately, anyway)—
We panicked—hoped this cryptic script related
Not to our scurrilous words and lives, but the mead
We had over-consumed. Yet this theory was hardly heartwarming;
However vague was our memory of wisdom writings,

This wall-scrawl wasn't nonsense, and we knew it.
In our lifetime we'd seen nothing so alarming
As these illegible, emphatic tidings
Of doom: whatever we had done, we'd rue it.

I

> "MENE: God has numbered your kingdom, and finished it."
>
> —DAN 5:26

When stoned or plastered, we still prayed to a giver—
Some deity, I mean—of stone or lumber,
Perhaps; but pleasure was our gold of gold,
And vanity our divinity of silver.
We counted out our cash, but could not number
Our violations of the laws of old.
Till those dogmatic digits made us quiver,
We didn't give a thought to moral slumber.
We ate and drank and sinned, and bought and sold
Our souls, equating joy with wealth, but never
Enumerating evil's final sum, or
Subtracting folly from our heathen world.

II

> "TEKEL: You have been weighed in the balances, and found wanting."
>
> —DAN 5:27

How heavily our hardened conscience weighs

On us—as heavy as the gods we made
Of bronze and iron and our egos. Flaunting
Our pride, we bowed to offer drunken praise
Like King Nebuchadnezzar on parade.
(We should have learned from him, who was left haunting
A bestial no-man's-land, and had to graze
Until he knew the god to be obeyed—
The One who'd weighed him, and had found him wanting.)

III

> "PERES: Your kingdom has been divided, and given to the Medes and Persians."
>
> —Dan 5:28

Not even half-prepared for the incursion,
Our brains soaked through with mead and sheer conceit,
Intoxicated by pride, we had denied
Our unguarded state. This profited the Persians
And Medes. The quotient of our self-deceit
Left no remainder for us to divide.
The gluttonous bacchanals which had been our version
Of life, only added up to our total defeat:
By all calculations, our souls and our nation had died.

Postscript

If these fingers had written our verdict in our own language,
We couldn't have read the sentence, or done the math;
Our hearts were as hard as the wall where the words were engraved,

Our minds were like flint. We would have missed the message
If it hadn't been vehement. Any divinity's wrath
Was a thought we'd suppressed; we'd no notion how depraved
Were our sedimentary layers of sacrilege—
The cement of self-worship had hardened our culture to death;
Is it possible that, by this Writer, we could have been saved?

Addendum

> "... I will put my law in their minds, and write it on their hearts ..."
> —Jer 31:33

Whatever god you are, who writes your sentence
On walls where heathens quiver trying to read it,
If you have any mercy, give repentance
To us; translate your law, and make us heed it.

Whatever higher power, whose equation
Can solve the problems of our wasted nation,
Allow the aftermath of your invasion
To lead us to your singular salvation.

II

Revealed

*The Things Concerning Himself:
Old and New Testament Links*

"And beginning at Moses and all the Prophets, He expounded to them in all the Scriptures the things concerning Himself."

—Luke 24:27

"the mystery which has been hidden from ages and from generations, but now has been revealed to His saints."

—Col 1:26

THE BREATH OF LIFE: DRY BONES IN THREE MOVEMENTS

> "Prophesy to the breath, prophesy, son of man, and say to the breath, 'Thus says the Lord God: "Come from the four winds, O breath, and breathe on these slain, that they may live."'"
> —Ezek 37:9

I: Genesis

It starts with breath. Without it there's no life.
The bodies made from Paradise's ground
Were soul-less—couldn't move, or make a sound,
Till God breathed into Adam and his wife.

II: Prophecy

Offspring of Adam, buried in this ground
Made barren by your sins' tenacious weeds,
Can bones like yours be animated—bound
With flesh that's soiled by your evil deeds?
You're made of dust, which just a tiny breath
Can scatter; but you're breathless. Even death
Cannot be smelled in this dry atmosphere
Where you have lain so long in lifeless air.

Could it be possible for you to come
To life, though you've been deaf and dead and dumb
So long that every bit of ancient mud
Around your grave has turned to dust? No blood,
No breath, no flesh, have clothed your skeletons
Since you breathed air at least a century
Ago. Since they're besieged by entropy,
Could gale-force winds now animate your bones?

III: Resurrection

He breathed on his disciples. Then he said,
"Receive the Holy Spirit." And they were
Transformed—as if, till now, they had been dead
And, finally, now, they lived! The very air
They breathed was made of love for him, and for
All people, since he loved them. Where, before,
They thought his death was final, they realize
That they will some day follow him, and rise.

HOW SHALL THIS BE?

> "Then Abraham fell on his face and laughed, and said in his heart... 'shall Sarah, who is ninety years old, bear a child?'"
>
> —Gen 17:17

> "Then Mary said to the angel, 'How can this be, since I do not know a man?'"
>
> —Luke 1:34

I: Abraham

How can this be? You know my wife is barren;
It's been her theme for nearly all her life.
She's nagged me till I'm deathly sick of hearing
Her whining voice. It cuts me like a knife.
We've prayed—of course we have—to no avail. Her
Belief that life is meaningless without
A child, is proof to her that I'm a failure.
How can this be? And why now? There's no doubt
It would have greatly helped our dismal marriage
If this had happened sooner. Now, at our age,
Can we renew our romance, even after. . .
It's laughable. She'll laugh. We'll call him Laughter.

II: Joseph

How can this be? We haven't come together,
Mary and I. And I can't imagine
That she . . . I have no clue about the father.
Having been assured she was a virgin,
I fear it seems I have no other course
To follow, than pursue discreet divorce—

But, I've just had an overwhelming dream
That's made me both bewildered and relieved:
An angel told me Mary has conceived
The Inconceivable, who will redeem
Our people, and be King of Israel!
Who would have guessed Isaiah's prophecy
Had any role in it for one like me?
We'll call him "God With Us"—Emmanuel.

NUNC DIMITTIS

> "And Israel said to Joseph, 'Now let me die, since I have seen your face, because you are still alive.'"
> —GEN 46:30

> "Lord, now you are letting your servant depart in peace, according to your word; for my eyes have seen your salvation..."
> —LUKE 2:29–30

I. Israel (Jacob)

Now let me pass away in perfect peace—
The son I've loved and lost is still alive!
I've thought my sorrowing would never cease;
But in my age, once more I can embrace
You, and it is enough; I will not grieve
Again. I'll gladly go now to my grave,
Grateful to God for unexpected grace.
Now let me die, since I have seen your face.

II. Simeon

Lord, all these years, I've prayed you to relieve
My restlessness to see this One whom I've

Been waiting for. I am content to leave
The earth, now that your mystery's been unsealed.
At last, I can beseech you to receive
My aged soul in heaven, where none grieve,
And all will see the One you have revealed.
I've held your Son; my life is now fulfilled.

**IF YOU ASK FOR BREAD,
WILL HE GIVE YOU A STONE?**

— Matt 7:9

I

Tempting Eve, the serpent said,
"Don't fast from this attractive tree;
Gain food and knowledge here, instead.
Do as I say, and you'll be free."

II

Tempting God, the people said,
"We cannot live on words alone.
These laws inscribed on slabs of stone
Can't feed us. How can rocks be bread?
And after all, look now—not one
Law's left upon another—Moses
Got so mad he threw them down.
They're smashed! Aren't you the God who knows us?
Don't you know we'll soon be dead
If you won't feed us? Can you hear?
Are you stone-deaf? What kind of God

Would kill us in this desert, where
We're starving? Are you really there?"

III

Attempting bribery, Satan led
The Second Adam to some bread-
Sized stones; and when this Adam said
He didn't live by bread alone,
The tempter tried a bigger one—
The temple. "Go ahead—jump down!
Let angels save you. Everyone
Will certainly adore you then!"

He didn't. Nor would he bow down
To gain with ease the worldly throne.

In forty fasting days, the Son
Broke neither law, nor fast, nor bone,
(Nor dashed his foot against a stone)
And by fidelity has shown
Man doesn't live by bread alone.

The Fall and desert are undone.
By dueling death, the Christ has won.

TWO VARIATIONS ON
THE THEME OF CHRIST'S BRIDE

> "The Church is in Christ as Eve was in Adam . . . God made Eve of the rib of Adam. And His Church He formeth out of the very flesh, the very wounded and bleeding side of the Son of man."
>
> —Richard Hooker

Creating man from dust,
And woman from his side,
God became the priest
At Eve and Adam's wedding.
He espoused them in a garden,
Then gave to them the best
Of gifts: the whole of Eden,
One tree alone forbidden.
But, still unsatisfied,
The bride and groom denied
His sovereign jurisdiction,
And made the doomed decision
To call his mandate void
And make themselves as God.
Having lost the perfect garden,
Their subsequent begetting
Would leave descendants sweating,

And cause the wounding of their Maker's side.

He'd made them in his image;
But in their fatal pride
They caused the deadly damage
For which the countless cost
Was that his love be crossed:
His Son, the Bridegroom, must
For them and us, their heirs, be crucified.
Yet, from his bleeding side,
He formed the Church, his bride,
Whom he still loves, and wed at Pentecost.

FOUR VARIATIONS ON THE CROWN OF THORNS

> "Cursed is the ground for your sake; In toil you shall eat of it All the days of your life. Both thorns and thistles it shall bring forth for you..."
>
> —Gen 3:17–18

> "When they had twisted a crown of thorns, they put it on His head..."
>
> —Matt 27:29

I

When Adam first was clothed, and cursed with thorns,
And Eden's weeds around earth's laureled head
Took root and spread,
Creation's gown was torn,
Her crown of foliage warped into a coil
That wormed its way into the garden's soil,
Invading earth's corrupted core
With twisted thistles keen to choke and spoil.
The decomposing world, without delay,
Was robed in mourning for
Her own decay.
And thus were Adam's kin

Continually tangled in
The stranglehold of sin.

II

From heaven to this garden's gnarled bed
The Second Adam came, prepared to tread
Its thorn-choked path,
Took all the world's sharp briars on his head,
Drank bitter wine from grapes of heaven's wrath.
No other Man but this one could unwind
The wretched wreath, and free mankind
From earth's deep-rooted entropy.
Unweaving thickets of iniquity,
He bound Himself to crucial misery,
His sacrificial head hard-pressed
With thorns. Distressed
With loss of blood and friends' desertion, he
Slashed through all barriers to Calvary.

III

The Gardener who's intimate with grieving
Arrives at the disastrous scene, unweaving
Parched vineyards, tearing weeds and weeding tares,
Removing overgrowth of envy, snares
Of avarice, depravity—roots curled
In thorn-corrupted dirt of a grasping world.
From these, pulled from the garden's knotty bed,
His foes have fashioned for his guiltless head

A crown which he accepts and gladly wears
For guilty humankind, though it was hers.
He feels all evil pierce his godly skull;
Forsaken, faces Golgotha's tart gall.

IV

Despised, rejected, all uncomeliness,
The Word-made-mankind's-champion runs his race,
Breaks through thick paths of thickets serpentine
With sin. His torn hair, lacerated face,
And sweat-drenched, soil-streaked, abraded skin,
Are imaging an unkempt, fallen world.
With bleeding feet, he treads tough roots and gnarled,
Malevolent vegetation, brittle vines,
And brambles berried with blood-beads from his veins.
He crushes twisted twigs and tares, untwines
Creation from the Fall-contorted crown
That Adam's kin have weaved of overgrown
Lust, envy, pride, and every kind of vice.
He takes their wreath, gives them his righteousness,
Calls them his branches, and himself their Vine
And, from his veins, gives them his perfect wine.

THE LAMB

> "And Abraham said, 'My son, God will provide for himself the lamb...'"
> —Gen 22:8

> "Behold! The Lamb of God who takes away the sin of the world!"
> —John 1:29

The Lamb has been provided. Here he is.
This time no substitute is in the thicket,
This time no sudden angel to hold back what
The Father's arm will do—no voice that says
To stop before the deed is done—because
This Lamb will battle death by death, and break it.
Before all time, the plan had been decided.
He's here right now. The Lamb has been provided.

ARE YOU THE COMING ONE?

> "Are you the coming One, or do we look for another?"
> —Matt 11:3

I

Isaac—unexpected, long-awaited,
Both comfort and uncanny irony
To your bewildered, ninety-year-old mother
Whose body has been suddenly invaded
Absurdly by a force miraculous—
What prophecy
Have you to tell us of another
Child of impossibility?
You are the unanticipated voice
Of Sarah laughing in the wilderness,
Her sudden half-belief
A comical relief
From vexing years of bitter barrenness.
Unwittingly, you are the incarnation
Of inconceivable anguish: Abraham
Sickened, desperately looking for a lamb
To take your place, horrified by the price
He must pay: making you a sacrifice.

Though Abraham truly was your father,
You showed the world it waited for another.

II

Samson, judge condemned to always wrestle
Both with the Philistines and pharisaical
Men of your own country who were jealous
Of your superior muscle,
Your superhuman prowess,
What light can your bizarre adventures cast
Upon the future, stronger Judge who lost
His life to kill not Philistines, but Death
Itself?
Your strength of body, his of spirit, both
Came with the curse of envious enemies—
Fierce Philistines and two-faced Pharisees—
And traitor friends. You ripped the city gate
From its foundation, bore it on your back;
Then, out of vengeance, threw your weight
Against the thieves who stole your eyes:
Stood cruciform between two pillars,
Made the temple crack—
Glad to make yourself a sacrifice
To crush the ones who'd been your cruel jailors.
And though you died for malice, He for love,
You did portend the greater Judge to come,
Whose sacrificial death would save
His enemies from such a doom.
The crossbar put upon him by his killers
Caused all creation's bedrock, all earth's pillars,

To crack—
        yet he came here, not to attack
His human foes, but Satan's reign—replace
Us with Himself between the thieves, forgive our vice—
A wholly hateless sacrifice.

The prophets looked for one to save; but neither
Were you the one; they must look for another.

GOOD FRIDAY:
"LET ME DIE WITH THE PHILISTINES."

> "And Samson took hold of the two middle pillars which supported the temple, and he braced himself against them, one on his right and the other on his left. Then Samson said, 'Let me die with the Philistines!' And he pushed with all his might, and the temple fell..."
>
> —JUDG 16:29–30

> "Jesus, when He had cried out again with a loud voice, yielded up his spirit. And behold, the veil of the temple was torn in two from top to bottom; and the earth quaked, and the rocks were split..."
>
> —MATT 27:50–51

With the weight of the crippled world's crossbar against his spine
And blinded by blood in his eyes from the crown of thorn,
He is willing to die for the like of these philistines
Who find savage entertainment in taunts and scorn
Of him, their new Samson—exhausted and finally shorn
Of power. They brutally set him up in between
Two pilloried thieves, right and left—but behind this scene,
Unseen, are the pillars of Earth that this Judge was born
To break down—and at this same time to rebuild, where they fell,
His Church: the substructure of heaven and wrecker of hell.

STRANGE BLINDNESS: A PLAY IN TWO ACTS

Prologue

Joseph and Jesus knew that perfect timing—
and not plain, unforeshadowed proclamation—
would show the deepest truth about life's drama.
Its plot twists often need a drawn-out comma
for characters who need some preparation
before they can perceive the play's full meaning.

Act I

> "So Joseph recognized his brothers, but they did not recognize him."
>
> —GEN 42:8

As one long-dead to these eleven others,
omniscient Joseph leaves them blind. He sees
the past and future starting to converge,
as in his childhood dreams. Emotions surge.
His flair for improvising emerges, and frees
his mind to write new roles for these wretched brothers.
Having their sight restored would overwhelm
them at this point, and cut the drama short

of its potential power—would avert
its climax. So, with no apparent qualm,
he keeps contriving more suspenseful scenes
for them to act without knowing what the play means,
To show them a haunting, shadowed silhouette
of the truth they were determined to forget.

Act II

> "... Jesus Himself drew near and went with them. But their eyes were restrained, so that they did not know Him."
> —LUKE 24:15-16

Supporting characters don't recognize
the lead, who makes his re-entrance quietly
from somewhere far beyond the footlights' blaze.
During an intermission of three days,
the disillusioned audience has withdrawn,
assuming that the play had ended when
the lead had died. Not knowing night from dawn,
forgetting that the curtain's not been drawn,
eleven friends who should have known the script
are waiting in the wings, bewildered, dazed.
Too paralyzed by grief to see the signs
of rising day, they're fearful, unequipped
to play their parts, not knowing they have lines.
Two minor characters, in cameo,
oblivious that they are on a stage,
are joined by One whose speech comes from a page
they've read before; yet still they do not know

this one who'd left his friends three days ago.
He won't unblind them at this moment, though,
because to fearful eyes he needs to show,
not tell. They walk and talk until a change
of scenery: a table; breaking bread
with perfect timing, he unveils a strange
new vision of the Word who once had said
that they would see him risen from the dead.

MORBID JOKE

> "Scripture has foretold it, how one death the other devoured, a joke of death has been made."
>
> —Martin Luther, from Bach's Cantata 4, *Christ Lay in the Bonds of Death*

I: Pharaoh's Droll Dream

> "And the ugly and gaunt cows ate up the seven fine looking and fat cows. So Pharaoh awoke."
>
> —Gen 41:4

A group of well-fed cows, and one of thin,
Debated what to do in a famine.
A fat one said, "Though you
Look pretty hard to chew,
We might survive by living on your skin."
"A very morbid joke,"
A skinny bovine spoke.
"You must be quite a wag
To think of such a gag
(You'd gag on me!) but now I'm realizing
It's you who look a lot more appetizing."
The thin one tried her luck,
And somehow didn't choke

While gulping down her well-appointed kin.
The punchline of the joke:
She still was just as thin,
After this, as she had ever been.
There must have been some magic—
Or else she had a stomach
That was a glutton for the tragi-comic.

II: Satan's Surprising Nightmare

> "Death is swallowed up in victory."
> —I Cor 15:54, quoting Isa 25:8

I thought that It Was Finished, when my Foe
Declared it was; this much, at least, I know:
He certainly was dead!
I thought I'd done it: made the grave devour
My Enemy. He'd passed his crucial hour
And gone where all my demons fear to tread.
These past three days we've thrown a party, feasting
In celebration of his not existing.
I didn't have a clue;
Did I misconstrue
That thing his prophet said—
Some line, some kind of motto,
Like Victory would swallow
Up death? But that deceiver
Could have said whatever
He liked, and never made me a believer.
Yet now, his tomb is hollow.

As are my plans. There must have been more to it
Than what I thought I knew. I guess I blew it.

THE DONKEY'S PALM SUNDAY

> "Now the donkey saw the Angel of the Lord standing in the way with his drawn sword in his hand..."
> —NUM 22:23

> "They brought the donkey and the colt, laid their clothes on them, and set Him on them."
> —MATT 21:7

This noisy, crowded scene is so surreal,
It makes it seem that this is still my dream.
But whether I'm asleep or not, I feel
A sickened sense that something is amiss.
We beasts can sense our riders' moods; and this
Is one unhappy man—though it appears
These people love him—want to crown him king
Of something. Yet their manner seems demanding
(And his, sadly resigned.) I think their cheers
Hold something subtly savage: though they bless
With shouts, a secret curse is in them. (Yes,
Of course—how would I know? I'm just an ass.)

My lowly line of sight is filled with smears
Of people's clothes and soft leaves shaped like swords.

They jog my memory: I dreamed I heard
My ancestor—the famous one, who halted
And knelt before the Angel with a sword,
Saving his man from death. Unfairly faulted
For stopping as they headed, hellbent, toward
A sinful scheme (his reckless rider blamed
My forefather for seeing what he couldn't),
He spoke in human language! Anyway,
He spoke last night, to someone, as I dreamed—
Called something to this frightening effect:
"Have nothing to do with that just man," he said;
"Whatever they want you to do, I'm sure you shouldn't."
If this was meant for me—I'm quite perplexed—
Then where's the Angel standing in my way?
Yet something here is crucially askew.
I want to stop—to press my side into
This wall of people whose ferocious fervor
Has caused my rider's dread; I feel him shiver!
But if I stopped, what would these people do?

They must have lost their minds to have such passion
For one who won't accept their acclamation.
Their crazy zeal supports my premonition
Of tragedy. If only I could speak,
I'd ask him who he is, and why he's come.
Is this a nightmare? Oh, please let me wake!
I want so much to ask him—but I'm dumb.

EASTER MORNING: EARLY RISERS

> "Then the king arose very early in the morning and went in haste to the den of lions."
>
> —Dan 6:19

> "Very early in the morning, on the first day of the week, they came to the tomb when the sun had risen."
>
> —Mark 16:2

Torn between horror and hope as the night was dying,
Darius runs to the den with guilt and dread.
Taking no burial spices, his hope defying
All logic, he seeks Daniel's life in the place of the dead.
For though he's a king, in spite of heroic endeavor
He has no power to roll away the stone
Which his pride has sealed as law—but all is undone
As he hears from the mouth of the grave, "King, live forever!"

Their hearts torn by sorrowful love as the sun is rising,
The women, pondering on the immovable stone,
Find their mouths wide open , reflecting the tomb's surprising
Disclosure of bareness—their Lion of Judah gone.
Prepared with the burial spices, they're unprepared
For the angel's announcement, which makes them gasp and shiver

With fear and with joy for One greater than Daniel, who dared
To look into death's mouth—their King, who now lives forever.

PARTINGS

The God who with his power created
Earth and Heaven, who also parted
Land from sea
And separated
Sea from sky, later divided
One sea into two, to free
The people he had multiplied
From Pharaoh's cruel tyranny.
With liquid walls on either side,
They sped between, their feet still dry.
And then the waters reunited
And the sea reflected sky
Again. By fire and cloud,
God guided
All that crowd.

And now, the God who parted waves
To free his people who were slaves
So long ago—
Who let them go
Into a land where milk and honey flow—
Is parting clouds as he receives
His Son, in triumph. As he leaves

His friends, they see
Death swallowed up by immortality:
The One who had been crucified
And in the grave
Will be alive
Forever. As they watch the tidal wave
Of cloud divide—
The sky reflecting foamy sea—
It takes their Lord, whose reign extends
To every place, both low and high,
Through sea and earth and sky.
Now, bodily,
His earth-time ends.
They both rejoice and grieve as he ascends.

III

Fulfilled
It Is Finished: New Testament Stories

> "Then He said to them, 'These are the words which I spoke to you while I was still with you, that all things must be fulfilled, which were written in the Law of Moses and the Prophets and the Psalms concerning Me.'"
> —Luke 24:44

> "Yes, and all the prophets, from Samuel and those who follow, as many as have spoken, have also foretold these days."
> —Acts 3:24

CHRISTMAS WITH THE ANIMALS

The God who feeds the world was once content
To sojourn in an ordinary stable—
To be confined to swaddling sheets, unable
To feed himself. In this inelegant
Retreat, the Word is eloquent, surrounded
By common beasts unwittingly attending
His nearly noiseless yet profound descending.
Unheard by the world, though his angel choir sounded
Around him, here among the cows and sheep
And in their borrowed trough, he's mooed to sleep
By dirty beasts that voice with ignorant grace
Their rustic song in this ignoble place.

THE SHEPHERDS OF THE NIGHT

The shepherds of the night by starlight come,
From watching sheep, to see God's newborn Lamb
Stabled with beasts, and swaddled from the cold:
The infant Shepherd David had foretold.

Wise men and humble kings, led by a star
To David's city, find his royal Son
In Bethlehem at the appointed hour—
The king of kings, wiser than Solomon.

Oh Lamb of God, Good Shepherd of the fold,
Lead your flock always in your path of light.
Incarnate Wisdom, King of all the world,
Rule in our darkness. Shine into our night.

"AND THE DARKNESS DID NOT COMPREHEND IT."

—John 1:5

This light that shines in darkness can't be seen
By worldly wisemen who have long preferred
Their hell-lit pride; this heaven-spoken Word
Means nothing to their ears, because the din
Of all the envious, self-seeking world
Has deafened them. Though all the earth is whirled
By this strange birth, they won't adore this Child
Whose kingdom they can't enter. They've reviled—
Not wondered at—the God-with-mortal-skin.
While angels dance, their darkened egos spin
Demonically; while stars sing, they are in
Denial of divinity. They turn
Their God-made sight away from him, and spurn
Their Maker, stop their ears, will not discern—
With blinded eyes and purposely dull ears—
The one true Word, in which true light appears.

SORDID SIGNS

Among the moan of kine and smell of sheep,
The plaintive whine of fowls half-asleep,
A woman in the throes of Eve's distress
(Who never chose this charge, yet answered "yes")
Now gasps in pain; and here among the cold,
Chaotic air of Adam's night grown old,
God's Son arrives among such sordid signs,
Concealed in Heaven's earth-and-straw designs.

THREE TRIPTYCHS

Time is traversed by eternity:
God in our human heredity
Lies between Joseph and Mary.

Shining, transfigured, the locus
Where earth meets the heavens, Christ glows as
He speaks with Elijah and Moses.

Thieves hung nearby him on either side,
Innocent anguish personified,
Jesus, between them, is crucified.

THREE DAYS

I

"... after three days they found Him in the temple..."
    —Luke 2:46

"... a sword will pierce through your own soul also..."
    —Luke 2:35

We've looked for you for three days, sorrowing,
Molested by one fear and then another.
How could we lose our son? It's harrowing
(Though all will call me blessed) to be your mother.
Three days we've hurried back against the bustle
Of carefree crowds returning from the feast.
They're glad with wine, unconscious of the jostle,
As we press past them on our worried quest
To find you. I think, sometimes, that we both
Most often find that we are going south
While everyone around us pushes north.
I guess we should have known where you would be—
But, unlike us, you always seem to know
Just where your unseen Father leads; you go
His cryptic way, seeing what we can't see,

Hearing the voice your human family
Can't hear. I treasure all you say, and ponder
These things; but I can't save you from your goal.
These three grim days have been a stark reminder
Of Simeon's sword. It starts to stab my soul.

II

> "The Son of Man must . . . be killed, and be raised the third day."
> —Luke 9:22

We've sat here, pale as specters, sorrowing
For three days, though you told us you would rise—
Not as a ghost, but human—narrowing
The gap between the God who never dies
And mortals, who can't comprehend this thing.
We should have been aware, should have believed
That you, the Son of God, could not stay dead;
But, seeing what the nails and spear achieved,
We couldn't stop the nightmares; saw the blood,
Heard violence each time we closed our eyes:
The hammered nails, the diabolic lies
Pierced through our souls. Three harrowing, hellish days
We felt our horrid helplessness, a haze
Of sorrow, anger, fear. Now yesterday's
Distress dissolves in shock, as if sunrise
Quite suddenly cleared midnight from the skies
And mourning from our hearts. Soon now, its rays
Will set the souls of many more ablaze.

IF YOU ARE THE SON OF GOD

> "... And the stone that struck the image became a great mountain and filled the whole earth."
> —Dan 2:35

> "If You are the Son of God, command this stone to become bread."
> —Luke 4:3

Now that you have lasted forty days
Without your Father's promised daily bread,
Dare you, the Rock of Stumbling, give offense
To me, when I have generously shown
And offered you a tempting feast of stone?
Where is this Bread of Heaven? Has God said
He will supply your needs?
                              Well then, instead—
If you can't live on such small rocks alone—
Here is the temple. If you are the Son
Of God, come down. Your foot (has not God said?)
Will not be dashed against the cornerstone.

The temple isn't big enough? Well, then,
One offer more: this mountain for your own—
Yea, all the world! Now, since you have not thrown

Yourself down from the temple, gain your throne
By falling at my feet. Has not God said
One knee will not be left that's not thrown down?
You shall not surely die, but be as God.

What? I give you offense? You're not inclined?
Why is your face so lined with anger? Whence
This rudeness? Get me hence? Get me behind
You? What am I—a serpent? Will you bind
Me up in knots? Why should you take offense?
Is this the thanks I get for such a kind
And lavish offer?
              Well, then, never mind.
I've overstayed my welcome; I'll be gone.
But at some more convenient time I'll come.
I'll have you in the end—or be undone.

ONLY ONE WINS THE PRIZE

> "For an angel went down at a certain time into the pool and stirred up the water; then whoever stepped in first, after the stirring of the water, was made well of whatever disease he had."
>
> —John 5:4

> "Do you not know that those who run in a race all run, but one receives the prize? Run in such a way that you may obtain it."
>
> —I Cor 9:24

"It's starting—on your mark, get set, and go!
The first one in the pool will get the prize!"
They've waited many days; they never know
Just when the swirling water will surprise
Them; when it does, it's time for them to rise
And hobble, stumble, limp, or even crawl
Until they hear a splash. (It could be comic,
If it weren't sad, to see these racers fall
Competing with each other.) Such ironic
Defeat they feel: they can't get in the pool,
Since they're infirm and feeble; most can't run
(Or even walk.) And, since they can't get in,
They'll never run. One winner; that's the rule.
The poignancy is palpable—for one

Especially, whose lameness has been chronic
For nearly forty years. The others shun
Him for his constant whining, and his panic
Whenever each new race begins. His eyes
Begin to dart about; his voice, pathetic:
"I have no friend to help me in!" he cries.
"It isn't fair! Is no-one sympathetic?"

Here's someone new . . . They think he's come to mock
Them all. He asks this man what seems a cruel
Question: "Do you truly want to walk?
If so, you need my help. Forget this pool."
And then, to everybody's total shock,
"Stand up!" And he was up. We saw him walk.

THE MAN BORN BLIND

> "The people who walked in darkness have seen a great light."
> —Isa 9:2

> "Since the world began it has been unheard of that anyone opened the eyes of one who was born blind."
> —John 9:32

The dawn foretold in prophecy,
The sun's new incarnation, is in view;
For those with sightless eyes begin to see
Salvation's light, which makes all vision new.

The stars declare the prophets wise
Who saw the dayspring's rising revelation.
Now Gentile wise men see the Christ-star rise
To heal the blind and make of them a nation.

The sunrise of epiphany,
The newborn vista, casts its royal hue
On Gentile kings who come with gifts to see
And kneel before their King, the infant Jew.

The world's true Light, preceding sight,
Who formed man's eyes, remolds them now with clay;
And things which once were hidden now are bright,
And those who walked in darkness see the day.

A PSALM FOR LAZARUS

> "Will You work wonders for the dead? Shall the dead arise and praise You? . . . Shall Your wonders be known in the dark? And Your righteousness in the land of forgetfulness?"
>
> —Ps 88:10, 12

Shall the dead rise up again and praise you?
How shall all your wondrous works be known
In darkness, shown
To one whose grave-clothed eyes can have no view?

Will your loving-kindness be forgot
By him who lies behind this senseless stone?
No light has shone
Where surely this man's flesh begins to rot.

Where are your wonders? Have they turned to naught?
Your righteousness and truth—do they still live?
And we who grieve:
Must we be shrouded now, in clouds of doubt?

Shall the grave declare your faithful ways
To those inside the earth who lie alone
Where not a bone
Can feel your sun's illuminating rays?

Yet this man must have heard your lordly shout,
"Lazarus, come out!"

JUDAS' KISS

> "Faithful are the wounds of a friend, but the kisses of an enemy are deceitful."
>
> —Prov 27:6

Bitter former friend, double-crossing kisser,
Did you fear losing face for staying faithful till the end?
Rabble-choosing voicer of greetings that pretend
Not to offend your Master—
Face him. Come closer.

See his face, hell-hounded: this nightmare day he's losing
All allies, yet refusing hostility. Though wounded
In heart, he still is choosing to love you while surrounded
By hate—while cruelly two-faced, Judas, you're abusing
His love; you boldly greet
Him with a rogue's deceit.

Tare in the field, you've grown among his crop of wheat.
Twelve men sat at his feet; but only to him were you known
As the one who held deceit as your right. You, alone,
Have turned on him with spite, ensuring your own defeat.
You've acted his enemy
Out of conceited envy.

So you devised this scheme, and now that you have handed
Him over, nails are pounded; you hear, and know your blame.
Among those who've demanded his death, yours is the name
That will be recollected long after he has bled.
And soon you will be dead, and not enjoy the fame
Of your infamous rude kiss,
Judas.

THIRTY PIECES OF SILVER

> "... So they weighed out for my wages thirty pieces of silver.... So I took the thirty pieces of silver and threw them into the house of the Lord for the potter."
>
> —Zech 11:12–13

> "Then [Judas] threw down the pieces of silver in the temple.... And they took counsel and bought with them the potter's field, to bury strangers in."
>
> —Matt 27:5, 7

Thirty silver pieces—
Worse than worthless, thrown
Down in sacred places—
Strike a guilty tone.
They echo two disgraces:
The price of a common slave
For God's only Son,
And men who want his murder.
Full of hate, and armed
With clanking swords and staves,
They follow the duplicitous,
Envious deserter
(Chosen by the Potter,

Now too hard to be reformed).
He has let resentment fester
Until, against his Master,
He comes with cruel kiss
That stings more than the thorn
That will pierce through skin to skull;
Then wishes, after this,
As silver coins roll,
That he'd never been born.

Thirty silver pieces
Roll, clang, clatter
Like shrill, prophetic voices.
Could they preach to the litter
In the house of the potter—
The broken clay shards
Misshapen, too hard
To be re-formed—would
They have called out the traitor
Who had thrown his own soul
On the wreckage, as they
Continued to roll
And the potter threw his clay?
Thirty silver pieces:
The dreadful deed is done.
Exposed to the disgraces
Of sorrow, blood, and scorn,
God-as-villain faces
Agony alone.

TWICE AND THRICE

> "... even this night, before the rooster crows twice, you will deny Me three times."
> —Mark 14:30

Though all shall be
Offended, I will not.
Though I should die
I will remain with thee
Until the end.
No—no alarming cock
Will dare deny
My loyalty. The thought
Of You, my friend,
Without myself—your rock—
Well, have no doubt.
These others—never I—
May say they know you not
And leave you, but
Three thousand roosters never could entice
Me to abandon you—so don't think twice.

TRIOLET: FEAR, FRIENDS, SHEEP

> "... Then all the disciples forsook Him and fled."
> —MATT 26:56

All his friends forsook him then, and fled
(All we, like frightened sheep, have run away)
While he hid not his face from shame, but bled
For friends (both them and us) who shook and fled.
We've quaked with fear of earthly powers, instead
Of fearing the Almighty. We and they—
His friends—denied, betrayed, forsook him—fled,
Like frightened sheep who all have gone astray.

CHRIST BEFORE PILATE

> "And with a mighty meaning of a kind
> That tells the more the more it is not told."
> —Edwin Arlington Robinson, "The Sheaves"

The power lies in what is left unspoken.
The Word-Made-Flesh stands mute; he's been forsaken.
Uncannily, his silence—even denser
Than chief priests' hatred, or their lawless plot
To kill this rabble-rousing crowd-entrancer—
Dumbfounds the governor. Truth's deepest answer
Cannot be heard by Pilate; he may not
Be used to weighing philosophic thought.
(Or, is he? Has he wondered, "What is truth?"
Before? His voice and face seem filled with both
Desire for such knowledge, and sarcastic
Expression.) But, what courteous or caustic
Response—what futile, incoherent phrase—
Could satisfy his crucial inquiry?

So, right back into those myopic eyes,
The Truth stares back the utmost irony.
He needs no words; the Word is what he is.
All other words are better left unspoken.

Though Pilate tries to wash his hands of truth,
He feels his self-assurance being broken.
He now knows he's not fit to judge for death
Or life, falsehood or truth, yet speaks death's sentence
On this true Word, who opens not his mouth—
Who signifies, in sacrificial silence,
The truth embodied, standing as its token.
His power lies in what is left unspoken.

PILATE'S WIFE

I've had a nightmare! Let that just man go!
You're right that he's done nothing wrong. They're wrong
To want him dead. No, nothing you could write
Above his head could possibly undo
Your guilt. He's innocent, however long
You try to wash your hands of him. That rite
Is cowardly, since you know what is true.
You've said yourself, the power is yours. So do
What's right. If you do not release him, know
That all the horror I beheld last night
Will fall on you.

THE ACCUSATION

> "Sitting down, they kept watch over Him there. And they put up over His head the accusation written against Him: THIS IS JESUS THE KING OF THE JEWS."
>
> —MATT 27:36–37

Absurdly accurate the accusation,
Though claimed unsuitable by mocking Jews—
Pilate's last barb to them: the declaration
That this is how they pay their King his dues.

Ludicrously laughable the choosing
Of Caesar as their sovereign (such a ruse
As Herod's hypocritical perusing
The magi's minds so piously for clues.)

Prophetically profound the imprecation
Called down by those who jealously abuse
Their King, and seal their excommunication
By claiming blood-guilt for all future Jews.

Scornfully satirical the crown
Of thorns, placed—on the surface—to amuse
His torturers, who goad him to come down,
Not fathoming his fierce fight to refuse.

Torturously tormenting the temptation
To leave the cross; relentless his refusing
To take their dare and make immense sensation
(Which only would be their, and all men's, losing).

Irreverently ironic the abusing
Of infinite supremacy suppressed:
Temporal powers confounding and confusing
Their impotence with might they'd never guessed.

Incredibly incongruous their jest,
Audacious their assumption that they've won.
The devil-king has done his spiteful best,
In spite of which Christ's rule has just begun.

COME DOWN

> "He saved others; Himself He cannot save. If He is the King of Israel, let Him now come down from the cross, and we will believe Him."
>
> —MATT 27:42

Himself he cannot—or he will not—save
From brutal boors barbaric as Barabbas
Who see this spiteful spectacle as fabulous
Amusement. Having spit on him, they rave;
They curl their cruel lips; they shake their heads as
He suffers, savor his agony like savages.
They're blinded to this poignant irony:
That nothing else but this Man's blood can salvage
Their own bloodthirsty souls, or save a vestige
Of their degenerate humanity.
If he were to surrender to this futile
Dare to prove his claim, and leave the cross,
It would be, for all men, no less than fatal.
He stays there not because he can't come down,
But out of love for all his merciless
False witnesses with our incongruous
Contempt of him, our loud and pitiless
Mockery. So, on his splintered throne
He hangs, pierced by the sharp ironic crown.

He will not save himself, and yet he will
Save us, by dying on his killers' hill.

VILLANELLE FOR VIOLINS

> "All they that see me laugh me to scorn: they shoot out the lip, they shake the head, saying, 'He trusted on the Lord that he would deliver him: let him deliver him, seeing he delighted in him.'"
>
> —Ps 22:7–8, KJV (as interpreted by G. F. Handel in *Messiah*)

They laugh, like Handel's mocking violins,
At him in whom is all my deep delight.
They jeer, who should be mourning for their sins.

Instead, the heathen rage with cruel grins;
And I—his Father—choose to let them smite
And laugh, like Handel's mocking violins.

The quintessential irony begins:
His vision's blurred with blood; they have no sight
To know they should be mourning for their sins.

He loves his murderers, although their chins
And lips shake shame at him; their mouths spew hate
And taunts, like Handel's mocking violins.

Their spiteful venom speaks of Adam's kin's
Appalling pride; my humble Son, in spite
Of scorn from these who mourn not for their sins,

Scorns earthly strength; by heaven's weakness wins
Reprieve for all who someday will delight
In him and, having mourned for all their sins,
Sing Hallelujah with Handel's violins.

EASTER, 2018: APRIL FOOL'S DAY

"If you're the Son of God, come down, you fool!"
So sang the dunces when they'd danced on Friday
Their jokers' jig. Indulging, on that High Day,
In fatuous abuse and ridicule,
Chief priests were unembarrassed to be cruel—
Revealed themselves as demon-clowns: "Why stay
Up there, Your Highness? Come down here, and rule!
Your Father has forsaken you; why pray?
If you are God, stand here, on your footstool.
Or is that crucial place your heavenly throne?"

Today, their mock-hilarity is gone.
They've been upstaged by a more clever Jester
Who's come to bring glad laughter to this Easter.

SEPULCHRE

> "And very early in the morning the first day of the week, they came unto the sepulchre at the rising of the sun."
>
> —Mark 16:2 (KJV)

As the sun comes up, the women see the sepulchre.
He—the one they loved—has been here three days. They're unsure
Who will help them enter with their spices (since the stone
Weighs a ton at least, and chief priests' guards have made it sure).

They, who've undergone Good Friday's agonies and horrors
Haven't slept, yet got here early, weary to the bone.
They have the kind of heartache that no human long endures;
Still, they've come to do their duty as their friend's embalmers.

Then they see the stone's been moved—and while they stare in wonder,
Stunned, unable at this startling moment to remember
What their Lord had said about his rising, and the number
Of days . . . One, then all three, look in, recalling Friday's thunder.

Mouths open, like the tomb, they see two angels sitting where
His body'd been. As if that weren't enough, a gardener—
Or somebody—appears. One throws her caution to the Sabbath
Wind, with her interrogation: "Have you moved him, sir?"

No imaginary tale—no mystery or myth—
Ever could compare with what would suddenly occur
To them that moment. Visions, dreams, nor women's intuition
Can rival this day's validation of what every human

Knows by instinct: death is not the final conqueror.
Now they know things never will again be as they were!
Their trembling joy defies all bounds of mortal man's sensation.
This—above all else—is perfect love that casts out fear.

EASTER MATINS: MEDITATIONS ON FABRIC, FLESH, AND STONE

> "And [Joseph] took [Jesus' body] down, and wrapped it in linen, and laid it in a sepulchre that was hewn in stone..."
>
> —LUKE 23:53 (KJV)

> "Then Simon Peter... went into the tomb; and he saw the linen cloths lying there, and the handkerchief that had been around His head..."
>
> —JOHN 20:6–7

I

The avalanche of thunder yesterday
That caused earth's core to quake—the anguished groan
That made her prehistoric pillars crash—
Are silenced. History's longest Saturday
Is buried in the vault of morning's dun
Sky that slowly softens midnight's ash
To kinder colors, as the line between
Night and day frays at its eastern hem. In
Uncertain start of light, a skeleton
Of tree, bereaved of bloom, begins to wave
Its branches in a dance macabre, above
The rocky riddle of a vacant grave.

II

The veil of Sabbath's vespers starts receding;
Matins' gauzy horizon absorbs the bleeding
That's spread from earth's deep puncture-wound, where stood
A beam with nailed crossbar of red-stained wood
Weighed down with limbs and ligaments of God.

Dawn's drapes are slowly opened. Branches, gilt
With sunrise, stitch themselves into the quilt
Of cotton clouds, as if they are designing
A tapestry by weaving heaven's lining
With cryptic script: cross-stitches that might spell
A secret they are restless to reveal.

III

Grief tears the women's hope; its threadbare seams
Seem past repair; late joys are tattered dreams;
Their hearts are frayed; their flesh feels dry as stone.
They walk as ghosts. The whispered undertones
Of breeze-blown dresses voice their silent groans,
Obscurely echoing, within the weave
(Unnoticed by the women as they grieve)
Some mystic threads of otherworldly things.

Above their pain, the sky-obscuring cloud
That's done its three-days' work as world-sized shroud
Is rolling west behind their silhouettes.
It pales and dissipates, exposing spring's
Soft lavenders and mauves, as daylight puts

Cloud-pebbles' shadows in their morning places.
Waking from Easter Even's mourning slumber,
The heavens' dome has changed its clothes from somber
Shades to flaming red and orange blazes,
Then rising pink that forecasts flushing faces.

IV

Becoming visible, his boulder-pall—
Not where it was—hints what this all might mean:
Perhaps it is the subject of the scrawl
The branches have embroidered on this scene.
The ray of dawn's gold needle, where the hem
Of land meets sky, spotlights this precious gem.
Rolled away by angels from its tomb,
It serves as curtain to the stage where all
That was or will be, finds its crucial meaning
In that which prophets told from the beginning.

Startled speechless, the women start to quake.
Impossible imaginations loom:
What would have seemed a fabricated tale
Until this moment, suddenly is real.
With open mouths, they stare: the open tomb
Mutely replies. They've not felt more awake
Before—yet feel as if they're dreaming—both
At once. They try to comprehend the scene.
Finding no flesh where he had lately lain,
They focus on the neatly-folded cloth,
And find themselves outside the three dimensions
They've always known, beyond the things their eyes

Can verify, experiencing sensations
Too deep for their five senses' limitations
To hold. This new reality denies
Death's finality.
                They realize
Their hearts had been, for three days, petrifying
To keep them living through the pain; the line
Between the soul and body is so fine,
They'd felt at moments that they, too, were dying.
Like fault-lines in earth's crust, unknown and narrow
Until they quake; or like the subtle line
Where flesh divides from spirit, bone from marrow,
The line between belief and doubt is lying
Unseen, but cracking.
                      Now a well-known voice
Distracts them from the riddle they've been trying,
Impossibly, to solve, as if it held
The greatest secret ever kept or told.
Could this soft-spoken gardener have rolled
The stone away, and moved him from this place?
Their minds' thick drapes are opening, and showing
The fault-lines in their fleshly way of knowing.
His voice now briefly turns their startled hearts
To stone, then back to flesh; sensation starts
To see. The sun comes up. In half-belief,
They drop their burial spices with their grief.
Their sight no longer draped in darkness, they
Can see the night explode in endless day.

ANTICLIMAX

Shouldn't that have been the end? He rose!
A happy end—the summit—history's
Inexorable purpose: It was his
Great strife complete, his dreadful battle won,
The war beyond all human victories.
Why wasn't that the final denouement?
Instead, the world continues in its woes;
They've grown and multiplied for centuries.
The triumph he accomplished here seems un-
Triumphant, leaving us to blunder on
Until the story's undiscovered close.
Though we keep praying that his will be done,
The earth seems governed by his enemies.
His judgments look to be most often crossed,
The resurrection's triumph nearly lost.

ANOTHER DOUBTING THOMAS

> "... Unless I see in His hands the print of the nails, and put my finger into the print of the nails, and put my hand into His side, I will not believe."
>
> —JOHN 20:25

Unless I thrust my brain into your mind
(As if my intellect were not insane
From being Adam's offspring) and can find
A list of reasons earth could not contain
For why the wicked prosper, to explain
The inner workings of your strange design—
Unless I see and feel, I will complain
And make St. Doubting Thomas' reason mine:
That I am human, and require sight
And sense to trust, for such is mankind's plight.

PETER'S EPIPHANY

> "In [the sheet lowered from heaven] were all kinds of four-footed animals of the earth, wild beasts, creeping things, and birds of the air.... What God has cleansed you must not call common."
>
> —ACTS 10:12, 15

A lion-sized sheet weighed down with meat
Unclean for any Jew to eat
Descends to Peter from the skies
With a disturbing word: "Arise,
And feast on Gentile beast and fowl cuisine."
Three times the dream recurred; what could it mean?
What Peter thought was common, God called clean.
Now God was calling him: "At my command
You're sent. I'll change your heart to understand
This scene you see with such confused surprise
As my all-wise, uncommon enterprise.
What's signified by this variety
Of common beasts, is my ordained decree:
That, since the Crucifixion crossed earth's time
With my eternal kingdom, what were two
Separate nations, now are one. Each Jew
And Gentile who believes in me has been
Made clean—and been made wise, like those who came

To see the Lamb of God in Bethlehem.
For this God-Man—this infant—was the same
As Judah's priestly Lion, who would tame
The beastly hearts of men. Henceforth between
You there is no division; you have seen
The One from whom your father Abraham
Descends, and both of you from him: I AM,
The God-Man who made Jew and Gentile kin.

WHAT FIRE IS THIS?

> "Then there appeared to them divided tongues, as of fire..."
> —Acts 2:3

> "Eye has not seen, nor ear heard, nor have entered into the heart of man the things which God has prepared for those who love Him."
> —I Cor 2:9, quoting Isa 64:4

What fire is this, that comes from heaven, not hell?
And what inspired breath
Which does not quell
These flaming tongues, but makes them sing on earth?

What language do they sing? What prophecy?
Their music tells us more
Of mystery
Than any mortal ear can fully hear:

A pledge of things to come, a sign and seal
Of what has been prepared
For us—more real,
Even, than these flames which, now and here,
This single day, have flared.
Their memory will

Keep igniting us, as we recall
This light, this warmth, until
The time past time, when we'll
Delight in it forever. Meanwhile, fanned
By overwhelming wind
And fire, we try to stand,
Dare to trust the glowing moment's thrill,
Illuminated by the Holy Ghost,
Gasping in the gust of Pentecost.

www.ingramcontent.com/pod-product-compliance
Lightning Source LLC
Chambersburg PA
CBHW071437160426
43195CB00013B/1938